HEROES OF FAITH

Volume II

DOUG GREENGARD

Taylor-Brooke Media Inc.
Slidell, LA

Heroes of Faith
Volume II
By Doug Greengard

Taylor-Brooke Media Inc.
3090 Gause Blvd, Suite 247
Slidell, LA 70461-4155

Copyright © 2006 by Doug Greengard

All rights are reserved. No part of this book may be reproduced or transmitted in any form or by any means. This includes but is not limited to electronic or mechanical duplication, photocopying, recording, or maintaining any part of this book on information storage and retrieval systems without written permission by the author. However, brief excerpts may be used for reviews.

Library of Congress Control Number
2005928602

Greengard, Doug/Heroes of Faith Volume II

ISBN 09765928-1-9

Cover design by Shereen LeCron

Printed in the United States

Acknowledgements

This book is dedicated to my father, Chet, who instilled in me the principle of perseverance and was a living example of what unconditional love is. He ran a good race until June, 2005. My mother, Marcia, continues to inspire me with her creativity. I couldn't have asked for more supportive parents.

Debbie, my wife, has been a tremendous source of encouragement and has provided invaluable insight and wisdom for this book and, more importantly, in my life. She has kept me focused on what is really important and is an incredible blessing to me and our sons, Nick and Tyler.

I'm humbled that James Brown, among the most prominent sportscasters, made room in his active schedule to write the thought provoking forward for this book. I have great admiration for him professionally, but even more for him personally. I aspire to be the man of character and integrity that he is.

Shereen LeCron amazes me with her computer graphics talents. Her design of the book cover exceeds, by far, my greatest expectations.

I'm extremely thankful for our "Heroes of Faith," who see the power of their platform and took the time to be interviewed for this book and our radio feature,

The Christian Sports Minute. The positive impact they can make on someone's life is incomprehensible.

Through the battles we all face, including the devastation we personally experienced during hurricane Katrina, there is only one true source of encouragement: God's promises. It's my hope that they become even more real to you as you read through the stories in this book.

Table of Contents

Foreword xi

FOOTBALL

1. Irving Fryar 13
2. Jay Feely 17
3. Trent Dilfer 21
4. J. J. Moses 25
5. Ernie Conwell 29
6. Kabeer Gbaja-Biamila 33
7. Curtis Martin 37
8. Mark Richt 41

BASKETBALL

9. Allan Houston 45
10. Derek Fisher 49
11. Ervin Johnson 53
12. Rod Barnes 57
13. Lisa Leslie 61
14. Jenny Boucek 65

BASEBALL

15. Lance Berkman 69
16. John Smoltz 73
17. Paul Byrd 77
18. Orel Hershiser 81

GOLF

19. Betsy King 85
20. Bob Gilder 89
21. David Gossett 93

OLYMPICS

22. Leah O'Brien-Amico 97
23. Catherine "Cat" Reddick 101

SOCCER

24. Matt Jordan 105

HOCKEY

25. Adam Burt 109

NASCAR

26. Darrell Waltrip 113

MOTORCYCLE

27. Ezra Lusk   117

HORSE RACING

28. Pat Day   121

FOREWORD

We all tend to hold in high esteem the one who has conquered. It dates back to the gladiators in Roman times and continues right up to our present-day athletes. Society is quick to notice those who have achieved success, particularly in the arena of sports.

Some of us want to wear their jerseys, walk like them, talk like them—to emulate them. As we continually see these sports figures on television and read about them in newspapers and magazines, they can become larger than life. Whether we like it or not, these sports icons have become our role models. Their influence can be tremendous—in either a positive or negative way.

That is why Heroes of Faith, Volume II, is such an inspiration. It is refreshing to read about sports figures who desire to set a positive example. Some of the biggest names in sports, profiled in this book, are conquerors who have built their foundation on a personal relationship with Jesus Christ. How wonderful it is to want to emulate these "Heroes" in their faith, the area of their life that has truly made them a great success. They have been blessed with a tremendous platform and, most importantly, understand that it is not to be used for their own glory, but for His.

Jesus Christ is the ultimate conqueror. As we watch these "Heroes of Faith" head into their battles, it is my prayer that we will be continually reminded to keep our focus on the One whom we should hold in the highest esteem. He has given the ultimate victory to anyone who believes in Him.

James Brown
CBS NFL Today Host

Chapter 1

IRVING FRYAR

Former National Football League Receiver

Jesus said to him, "I am the way, the truth, and the life. No one comes to the Father except through Me."

John 14:6 (NKJV)

Few players have enjoyed the type of on-field success that Irving Fryar experienced during his National Football League (NFL) career. Fryar, who was the first pick in the 1984 NFL draft and played for 17 years before retiring in 2000, left his mark as the fifth-leading receiver in league history. On the field, there was no opponent that the speedy, sure-handed receiver could not beat. But away from the limelight of the NFL, Fryar was fighting a losing battle where the stakes were life and death. "I was at the end of my rope," said the five-time All-Pro, who reflected on that day in 1990 when he cried out to God from a jail cell. "I had been in jail a few times; drugs, alcohol, marriage not right, family and personal life not right. I really believe, sincerely, that if I did not make the choice to allow Christ to come into my life in that jail cell that I probably would not be here right now. I would probably be dead."

Fryar decided to live his life for Jesus Christ from that day on. Since then, the former NFL standout has become an ordained minister and now spends his time sharing the Gospel that saved him from total destruction. "I don't tell people right and wrong just because it's right and wrong. I tell them because I know what different things and different ways of life will do to you," said Fryar, who played for New England, Miami, Philadelphia and Washington during his lengthy and highly-productive career. "People have a tendency to listen to me because I lived a lot of negative situations. I can tell them that Jesus is the way, the truth and the life and there's no other way to get eternal life except through Jesus Christ."

While the experience of that day in a jail cell was quite painful, Fryar can now look back on it with great thankfulness. Sometimes, he admits, you have to hit rock bottom before you see the way back to the top. "There's no better way of living than to have Christ in your life," he added. "I've lived it all and, believe me, there's no better way to live than a saved life; a life with Jesus Christ at the forefront, leading the way."

Chapter 2

JAY FEELY
New York Giants, Place-kicker

The LORD gives strength to his people; the LORD blesses his people with peace.

Psalm 29:11 (NIV)

Jay Feely has experienced the exhilaration of making a game-winning field goal. He has also faced the despair of missed opportunities. Through the ups and downs of placekicking, Feely, now with the New York Giants, has learned that football is a lot like life. "Whether you make the kick or miss the kick, God is always faithful and He is always there," said Feely. "God's always there to help pick me up."

Feely set several team records in 2002 while playing for the Atlanta Falcons, including the most field goals in a season. Yet, the pressure that comes with winning or losing games with one swift kick cannot be ignored. It is through his relationship with Jesus Christ that he is able to handle the situations he regularly faces. "I have been able to turn it over to Him and have total peace," added Feely, who was named to the All-Rookie team in 2001. "That's just a credit to God's peace and the peace that He gives you. My favorite scripture is Philippians 4:6-7, which says, 'do not be anxious for anything, but through prayer and thanksgiving, make your requests known to God and the peace that surpasses all understanding will guard your hearts and minds in Christ Jesus.'"

Feely has not always enjoyed this type of peace. During his freshman year at the University of Michigan, he suffered a season-ending leg injury after the second practice. It forced him to re-evaluate his life. "For four months, I really struggled to try and find something to fill that void because sports had always been there for me," Feely said. "I was partying and drinking trying to fill that void. Finally, I said, 'you know what, God? I'm just going to turn it over to You. I'm not going to hold anything back. I'm putting it in Your hands. Whether I ever kick again, I know You're in control.'"

Feely, much to the disappointment of his opponents, is once again kicking and now enjoys having the Lord in control. He knows that God's plan for his life is a lot better than his own. Feely affirms, "If He's in control, you're going to have a great life."

Chapter 3

TRENT DILFER
Cleveland Browns, Quarterback

And we know that all things work together for good to those who love God, to those who are the called according to His purpose.

Romans 8:28 (NKJV)

From the pinnacle of success to the depths of despair, Trent Dilfer, quarterback for the NFL's Cleveland Browns, has experienced it all. He has seen times of great triumph and even greater tragedy in both his professional and personal life. "God has become so much bigger through these times," said Dilfer. "His grace has abounded beyond anything I ever thought I could experience."

The Dilfer family continues to deal with the loss of their son, Trevin, who after battling a heart ailment, passed away in the spring of 2003 at the age of five. It was the type of experience that can leave many questioning God. "I've never stopped to ask why," added the veteran quarterback. "We just ask what He wants us to learn from this and how He wants to use this. He has been faithful times a million."

Dilfer's football career has been an emotional roller coaster. After Tampa Bay chose him as the sixth overall pick in the 1994 draft, Dilfer spent his first six years playing for the Buccaneers. There, he emerged as the team's second all-time leading passer and earned a trip to the Pro Bowl. In 2000, he joined

Baltimore and quarterbacked the Ravens to the Super Bowl XXXV championship. "Winning the Super Bowl was great and it was fun and I enjoyed every moment of it, but it's a small moment in time compared to the gift of eternal life and what we have in Christ," said Dilfer, who saw countless teammates left unfulfilled in the wake of Super Bowl success. "Nothing fills the void except Christ. People hear that all the time, but it's true."

Before receiving his title ring, Dilfer was released by the Ravens and was signed by Seattle. His tenure in Seattle was marked with several injuries and he was relegated to mostly a back-up role. "I believe that God has allowed football to go that way in my life so that I trust Him more," added Dilfer, who signed with Cleveland in the spring of 2005. "I have really struggled with pride throughout my life, and if football would have come easy for me I would not have followed Him and trusted Him the way I needed to. And He, by His love, has allowed me to go through some hard times so I would be dependent on Him completely."

Through it all, Dilfer seems to have found the

one teammate he can always depend on. His name is Jesus Christ.

Chapter 4

J.J. MOSES

Arizona Cardinals, Return Specialist/Wide Receiver

The LORD is my light and my salvation; Whom shall I fear?
The LORD is the strength of my life; Of whom shall I be afraid?
                    Psalm 27:1 (NKJV)

J. J. Moses, who stands only five-feet, six inches tall and weighs 180 pounds, finds himself in a modern-day version of the battle between David and Goliath every time he steps onto the football field. "David wasn't always the biggest, but he had faith in God," said Moses, wide receiver and kickoff return specialist for the Arizona Cardinals. "That's how I am with football. There are a lot of guys bigger than me but I have such faith in the Lord. God is the One who gives me my strength. He makes me not fear. Every time I get a chance, I read the Word of God. It encourages me in knowing what Christ has done for me. I just give it all I have because I know that He's got my back."

Just as David's faith continually resulted in victory, Moses sees a similar pattern when he faces the giants in his life. "He didn't bring me here for me to fail. He didn't bring me here to make me hate football. There's a reason and He gave me the desires of my heart, so I'm going to make the most of it, telling people about Christ and having fun."

While Moses has been having fun, it has been anything but that for those who have tried to catch the speedy, explosive runner who consistently ranks among the NFL's leaders in kickoff return yards. Because of his lack of size, Moses has always been perceived as being too small. After a standout collegiate career at Iowa State University, he was signed by Kansas City as a free agent in 2001 and spent part of that season with the Chiefs. He also spent a short time with Green Bay in 2002, followed by a two year stint with Houston. "All my life I have been doubted and all my life I've had to overcome obstacles," added Moses. "The only way I've overcome them is by believing in Jesus. He's given me the favor. He's put me in the right situations to do things. It's all because of Him that I'm here right now, I know it."

Moses doesn't let anyone or, for that matter, anything stand in the way of a possible touchdown. He has a similar philosophy about sharing the message of Christ with others. "You never know how many years or how many months I might be here playing football," said Moses. "What I do is let people know about

Christ. I talk about Christ. I try to tell people about what He's done and I try to be a witness, above everything, because that's what it's all about. Football's fun, but it's not life. What am I going to do when my football career is over with? That's what I'm realizing; He's my strength and He's who I have, even when I'm not in football."

Chapter 5

ERNIE CONWELL

New Orleans Saints, Tight End

But we all, with unveiled face, beholding as in a mirror the glory of the Lord, are being transformed into the same image from glory to glory, just as by the Spirit of the Lord.
2 Corinthians 3:18 (NKJV)

Ernie Conwell knows the thrill of hauling in a pass and taking it into the end zone for a touchdown. Conwell, tight end for the New Orleans Saints, enjoys this type of on-field success because of the time and effort he has spent to prepare for an NFL career. He believes the same goes for his life, which is committed to following Jesus Christ. "There are a lot of parallels of how you train athletically and how you prepare, focus, visualize and study at this level of the game, and your Christian life is the same," said Conwell, who left the St. Louis Rams to join the Saints as a free agent in 2003. "You understand that it's a battle. You understand that you have to prepare and study. You know that you have an enemy and you're not ignorant of his devices or his schemes. We study a game plan against a team. We should also study the devices that Satan uses to try to destroy us and interrupt us."

Conwell hopes to help the Saints win their first-ever Super Bowl victory after assisting the Rams in capturing the NFL's top prize in 2000. In possession of a Super Bowl ring, he has now set his sights even higher than earning the right to play in the NFL's version of the All-Star game, the Pro Bowl. "I've made a commitment that as much as I would like to be a Pro-Bowl player in the natural world, my cry is to be a Pro-Bowler in the spiritual realm," added Conwell, a second round draft choice of the Rams in 1996. "I want to be a Pro Bowl Spirit Man. If I can accomplish that, who knows what will happen down the road. Football is just gravy on top of that."

While there have been countless victories, there have also been challenging setbacks. It was through his faith in Christ that Conwell was able to overcome a career threatening knee injury in 1998 and continue playing football.

His athletic accomplishments date all the way back to the days of his youth in Kent, Washington. But Conwell cannot say he always followed God's game plan for his life. That changed during his senior year in high school. "The Holy Spirit just kept pounding on me," said Conwell. "It came to a point in my life, where I was going to have to make a decision. Either I was going to rebel against what I knew was the truth or else I was going to be a real Christian. I came to that point where I said, 'God, I want to totally surrender and commit all my being to You.'"

Chapter 6

Kabeer Gbaja-Biamila
Green Bay Packers, Defensive End

...so that Christ may dwell in your hearts through faith. And I pray that you, being rooted and established in love, may have power...to grasp how wide and long and high and deep is the love of Christ.

Ephesians 3:17-18 (NIV)

On the football field Kabeer Gbaja-Biamila shows no mercy to his foes. As one of the NFL's top pass rushers, his mission is to sack the opposing quarterback. At the conclusion of the 2003 season, the six-foot-four, 255 pound defensive end became the first player in Green Bay Packer history to notch 10 or more sacks in three consecutive seasons. The following year, he added an additional 13½ sacks and now stands second on the team's all-time list. While Gbaja-Biamila's great speed allows him to be almost merciless to those he lines up against, he is even quicker to share with others the grace of God that has touched his life in an incredible way.

"I was a Muslim when I came to the Green Bay Packers," said Gbaja-Biamila, a fifth-round draft choice in 2000 who was named to the Pro-Bowl squad in 2003. "I tried to do it myself for 22 years and realized that my ways weren't working. I heard about Jesus and I said 'let me try it His way.' It didn't change me overnight, but little by little He began changing me. And then I fell in love with Him to the point now where I just want to share my testimony with everybody about what Jesus did for me."

By following Jesus Christ, Gbaja-Biamila learned what it means to be saved by God's grace. Now he is focused on an increasingly deeper personal relationship with the Lord. "All I want to do is please Him," added the former San Diego State University standout, whose 33 career sacks are a school record. "I have to trust that He has the best for me. He loves me more than I could ever love myself, more than my wife could love me; more than my earthly father and I know he loves me."

There are occasions when Gbaja-Biamila does not have a great desire to play football. There are similar days, he says, in his walk with the Lord. The answer for both is the same. "You don't focus on what you see, you focus on the instruments," added Gbaja-Biamila. "The Bible is the instrument. We have to trust God's Word no matter if we feel like doing something or not. Obeying God has nothing to do with feelings. It's all about being in Him and obeying His commandments. I'm keeping my eyes on my first love and that's Jesus Christ."

Chapter 7

CURTIS MARTIN
NEW YORK JETS, RUNNING BACK

"For I know the plans I have for you," declares the LORD , "plans to prosper you and not to harm you, plans to give you hope and a future."

Jeremiah 29:11(NIV)

Running for touchdowns in the NFL was never really in Curtis Martin's plans. As a youngster growing up on the violent streets of Pittsburgh, Martin was too busy running for his life. "My life had been jeopardized so many times I thought I was just lucky. I thought I had escaped all those situations because I was a lucky guy," said Martin, who saw countless friends and family members killed during his youth. "One day, I had a dream and something in that dream told me I had to thank God for everything that He did for me."

And so, he did. Martin found the nearest church and thanked God in the only way he knew how. "I remember going to church and saying, 'Look God,' and I was still talking to Him like I was on the streets or something, like He was one of my boys, because now He is, and I just said, 'Look God, I don't know you or this Jesus dude that everybody's talking about but now I have a reason to live, and I want to live and if you save my life I will serve you.'"

Since that day when Martin gave his life to Christ he has faithfully, but not perfectly, served the Lord. "I've made a commitment to serve the Lord and there were times when I knew I wouldn't turn back. But I fell a lot of times and I still fall," said Martin, who regularly notches Pro Bowl honors and continues to climb toward the top of the NFL's all-time rushing list. "I have learned His love and His forgiveness. If I fall, I have no problem getting up. It's like the Bible says, 'a righteous man falls seven times and he gets up again' [Proverbs 24:16]. What makes him righteous is that he knows God is love and His forgiveness is so strong and God's purpose is so much bigger than our mistakes. The relationship I've come to have with Him, the intimacy that I have means more than anything to me. Football, fame, money, all that, it's all so minute compared to the peace and happiness I have inside."

In 1995, after his junior season at the University of Pittsburgh, the New England Patriots selected Martin in the third round. Martin admits that, at first, he didn't want to play professional football. It was his pastor who encouraged him to use the game as a platform to share his faith in Christ. "To me, football is just a stage that God has given me, a vehicle that God is using to have me impact lives. It means more to me to touch one person than to win the Super Bowl," added Martin. "To know that I have helped and led a person to Christ and his life is saved eternally means more than anything that the world can give me—anything."

Chapter 8

MARK RICHT

University of Georgia, Head Football Coach

Trust in the LORD with all your heart and lean not on your own understanding; in all your ways acknowledge him, and he will make your paths straight.

Proverbs 3:5-6 (NIV)

ark Richt has done a more than admirable job calling the shots for the University of Georgia Football team. In one of the toughest football conferences in the country, he has led the Bulldogs atop the Southeastern Conference standings and brought them near the top of the college football polls. In 2002, Georgia's 12 wins, including a victory at the Sugar Bowl, tied a school record.

In his personal life, however, Richt allows his Lord and Savior, Jesus Christ, to make the calls. "When you finally let Him be Lord of your life, that's when things really start clicking for you because the things of the world that we sometimes get caught up in really don't matter much anymore," said Richt. "All of our hope and faith is in Christ, and you say, 'all right Lord, tell me what You want and I'll do it.' Regardless of what it is, you will have a peace about things."

Richt has not always had this perspective. Before taking the helm at Georgia, he spent 15 seasons as an assistant coach at Florida State. There, under the watchful eye of the legendary

Bobby Bowden, Richt found himself profoundly influenced by Coach Bowden's strong faith. "I was 26 years old at the time," he said. "My life has really been blessed since I accepted Jesus as my Lord and Savior."

That does not mean that Richt's life is easy. It is his faith in Christ, and God's promises of hope, peace and joy that have sustained him. Now, as a head football coach, Richt has many opportunities to share the good news of the Kingdom with others, just as Bowden did and still does. "It is a great opportunity," added Richt. "I don't take being a role model lightly. It's easy to be a role model when my goal is to honor God with what I do. To live a life that is pleasing to Him is my goal. If I come close to that goal than there's a good chance that I will be a good role model."

Richt has always loved football. During his playing days at the University of Miami, he was back-up to quarterback Jim Kelly, whose illustrious NFL career led to induction into professional football's Hall of Fame.

These days, Richt is taking his snaps for the ultimate coach, winning games and, more importantly, souls for Christ.

Chapter 9

ALLAN HOUSTON
National Basketball Association, Guard (Former)

Then Jesus said to his disciples, "If anyone would come after me, he must deny himself and take up his cross and follow me."

Matthew 16:24 (NKJV)

Much like the strategy that went into preparing for a basketball game, former National Basketball Association guard Allan Houston learned how important it is to be equipped for the bigger game of life. "The more you have the Word of God in your heart, and the more you believe and trust it, the more you will be able to apply it to your life," said Houston, who was forced to retire in 2005 because of knee injuries. "I think it starts with time with Him. It starts with prayer and surrendering. One thing I've learned is that we have to live in a worship mode everyday, all day. That's what I try to do everyday is worship Him and be willing to do whatever He asks me to do."

Houston, a six-foot, six-inch shooting guard, played 12 NBA seasons, mostly for the New York Knicks. A two-time All-Star and member of the 2000 Olympic team, Houston was one of the league's best outside shooters.

Raised in a Christian home, he committed his life to Jesus Christ at the age of 16. Houston went on to play in college for his father, Wade, at the University of Tennessee where he became the school's all-time leading scorer.

In the 1993 NBA draft, Houston was selected by the Detroit Pistons with the 11th overall pick. Three years later after joining the Knicks, Houston began taking his faith seriously. A strong influence was the fellowship of former teammate Charlie Ward and a cousin of Houston's, who was living in New York at the time. Both shared scriptures with the NBA star.

"They would apply them to basketball," added Houston. "Sometimes the Lord reaches us in different ways and that's how He pulled me back into Him. It happened through people I trusted and cared about. In 1995 I really committed myself, denying myself [Matthew 16:24], taking up my cross to really follow Him. All that time in between I knew I had God's protection over my life but I really wasn't living my life for Jesus Christ. I was living it for Allan Houston and using God and Jesus as a backdrop."

No longer leaving his faith in the background, Houston is sure to make his Lord and Savior the main attraction. "God doesn't put laws in place just to be legalistic," said Houston. "He put them in for our own protection. When I understood my purpose, His plan for my life, that's when my love grew deeper for Jesus."

Chapter 10

Derek Fisher

Golden State Warriors, Guard

...for they drank from the spiritual rock that accompanied them, and that rock was Christ.

1 Corinthians 10:4 (NIV)

Through hard work, determination and applying the talents he has been blessed with, Derek Fisher's game has developed tremendously over the years. Fisher, a former Sun Belt Conference Player of the Year at Arkansas-Little Rock, was the Los Angeles Lakers first round pick in the 1996 NBA draft. While with Los Angeles, Fisher worked his way into the starting lineup and helped the Lakers win three straight NBA Championships from 2000 to 2003. "There's only one person who can have that type of impact on my life and that would be Jesus," said Fisher, who now plays for the Golden State Warriors.

In the same way, Fisher's walk with Christ has become more of, you might say, a fast-break. The six-foot, two-inch guard committed his life to Christ at a young age. Growing up in a Christian home afforded him the benefits of knowing Jesus as his Lord and Savior. "As I've gotten older, my personal relationship with Christ has grown," said Fisher. "Now I'm able to realize that He's the source of my strength and that's where everything comes from and starts- it's through Him. To play 100 games a year,

Gatorade isn't the only thing that's going to help you do that. You need to know the source and Jesus Christ is the source for me."

Fisher has accomplished much during his career, but that is not to say everything has gone perfectly or even close to it. There was a foot injury that sidelined him during part of the 2001 and 2002 seasons. "I know that I wouldn't have gotten through that and back to the point where I am without Him being there for me," Fisher said.

More than connecting on the game-winning shot or making a dazzling pass to a teammate, Fisher's goal is to allow others to see Christ in him. "It's a great feeling to know that people are paying attention," he added. "Not just to the way a guy performs or how many points he scores or what his athletic achievements are, but really the personal decisions that he's making in his life. Sports fans appreciate when you're a complete person. I think it's impossible to be complete without Jesus being the centerpiece where everything revolves around Him."

Chapter 11

Ervin Johnson
Milwaukee Bucks, Center

Abide in Me, and I in you. As the branch cannot bear fruit of itself, unless it abides in the vine, neither can you, unless you abide in Me.

John 15:4 (NKJV)

Ervin Johnson's life story is a remarkable one, to say the least. Several years after graduating from high school, Johnson grew eight inches and was bagging groceries in a Baton Rouge, Louisiana supermarket when he was discovered. Standing six feet and ten inches tall, it seemed only fitting that Johnson play basketball. An opportunity to walk-on at the University of New Orleans presented itself and Johnson, then in his mid-20's, jumped at the chance. Johnson's invitation was certainly not because of his ability to play basketball. Truth was Johnson could barely even catch a ball, let alone shoot one.

But things changed. Through a lot of hard work and determination, Johnson's skills developed through what was an almost supernatural transformation. By the time his college career was over, Johnson was the Sun Belt Conference's Most Valuable Player and not long after, was a first round pick in the NBA draft. "God is really good," said Johnson, now a center for the Milwaukee Bucks. "God has been taking care of me. I'm just really glad that I can stand here and tell you about it."

Johnson has earned the distinction of being one of the NBA's top defensive players and rebounders. That has not happened by simply talking about it. Johnson has had to prove it through his actions. He says we should live our lives as Christians in the same way. "People know what type of person I am and they know what I stand for," added Johnson, who lovingly shares his faith in Christ at every opportunity. "We ought to be able to persuade those people who are of the world to come to know Jesus Christ rather than them persuade you to come back into the world. Others should be able to distinguish between our attitude and the fruit we bear. If we bear good fruit, others will be able to see it. We have to stay connected to the vine."

Just as he has developed as a basketball player, Johnson has become even more serious about his walk as a Christian. He experiences the type of joy that comes only through a relationship with Jesus Christ. Now, his quest is for others to grab onto the power of the Gospel the same way he hauls in rebounds. "I am trying to be as real as possible so I can somehow make an impression with the people around me and bring them into the Kingdom," added Johnson. "God is really allowing me to touch people that I am around in this organization. I want to make an impact no matter where I go. Jesus and His disciples made an impact wherever they went. I just want to do the same."

Chapter 12

Rod Barnes

University of Mississippi, Basketball Coach

I will teach you about the power of God; the ways of the Almighty I will not conceal.

Job 27:11 (NIV)

University of Mississippi Basketball Coach Rod Barnes is the first to admit that winning games is not his top priority. This might seem surprising when considering that Barnes has led Ole Miss to the postseason four times since taking the helm in 1998. His finest season was 2001, when the Rebels compiled a school record 27 wins, advanced to the NCAA Tournament's "Sweet Sixteen" and he was named National Coach of the Year. The victories are sweet, but Barnes feels greater satisfaction from something far more fulfilling: having an emotional and spiritual impact on his players.

"It's a great opportunity," said Barnes, who spent five years as a Rebels assistant coach before being promoted to head coach. "I'm so thankful to the Lord that He would choose me to stand for Him. God continues to show Himself every day and He continues to bless me everyday. I feel so fortunate to have the opportunity to stand before people and let them know how good God is."

Barnes has earned the reputation of being someone who does just that. Shaken by the death of his father in 1992, Barnes decided to live a life fully committed to serving Jesus Christ. It has been an exciting and often demanding journey for him. "It's been so awesome," added Barnes, who was also an All-Southeastern Conference player with Ole Miss in the mid-1980's. "In just my own life, I've asked God to draw me closer to Him. It's been a molding, creating and carving of everything. I'm seeking His face."

Barnes has found that some of life's greatest lessons have come during difficult times. The 2003 season, which ended with the Rebels missing post-season play for the first time in six years, was one example. "This was a season that brought about so many different things," he added. "Through all the adversity and tough times He gave me peace and showed so much grace. I'm so thankful to Him."

As his faith in Christ has grown, he has found it easier to believe in God's faithfulness. Barnes reflects on God's promises, "He says, you just do the things that are possible and I'll handle the things that are impossible."

Chapter 13

LISA LESLIE

Los Angeles Sparks, Center

May I never boast except in the cross of our Lord Jesus Christ, through which the world has been crucified to me, and I to the world.

Galatians 6:14 (NIV)

Standing a towering six-feet, five inches tall, Lisa Leslie can be an intimidating presence on the basketball court. She led the Los Angeles Sparks to back-to-back Women's National Basketball Association (WNBA) Championships in 2001 and 2002. She also became the first in league history to be named Most Valuable Player in the regular season, during the championship series and in the All-Star Game. In 1996, the first time she helped lead the United States Women's Olympic team to a gold medal, she made a decision to achieve the same kind of success in her personal life. That is when she got serious about her relationship with Christ. "I've grown so much in my walk with the Lord since 1996. I think that was the turning point of when I started to go to church every Sunday and not just because I'm supposed to," said Leslie, who was also named league MVP after the 2004 season. "I enjoy going and listening to the Word and being excited about it."

Leslie accepted Jesus Christ as her Lord and Savior when she was just seven years old and was baptized while in high school. It was a bit later in life that she faced the struggles of living a Christ-focused life in a mixed-up, confused world. Her commitment to press into God's Word gave her a new understanding. "Not just doing it because it's a ritual or part of our religion, so to speak, but doing it because I love to do it and I'm happy to be there," said Leslie. "To feel the presence of the Lord is an amazing thing."

Leslie, who became the first player in WNBA history to score 3,000 points and is the league's all-time leader in rebounds, has allowed her relationship with the Lord to mold her on the basketball court. In 1998, Leslie and some of her teammates began saluting one another, encouraging each other to be soldiers for Christ. Unfortunately, it went a little too far when one of Leslie's opponents began cursing at her and saluting back at her. "That really hurt my heart because the salute was for something positive and she kind of turned it into something negative. Regretfully, I hit her because of that," said Leslie, who asked God to forgive her and apologized to her church congregation soon after. "I think I've grown so much from that experience. I'm glad it happened because there've been other situations where I've been able to turn away from things where I could've fought or really got into it."

Whenever she gets the chance, Leslie, the 1994 National Collegiate Player of the Year at the University of Southern California, shares her story with a captive audience of youngsters, many of them who dream of following in Leslie's footsteps. "I just express to them with a lot of prayer and faith I've made it," she said. "No matter what your situations are, being in the inner-city or broken homes, the Lord's grace is so amazing He'll cover you."

Chapter 14

Jenny Boucek

Seattle Storm, Assistant Coach

Let us not give up meeting together, as some are in the habit of doing, but let us encourage one another—and all the more as you see the Day approaching.

Hebrews 10:25 (NIV)

During her seven years of being associated with the Women's National Basketball Association (WNBA), Jenny Boucek (pronounced BOO-check) has bounced around nearly as much as a basketball. Currently an assistant coach with the Seattle Storm, she previously served on coaching staffs in Miami and Washington. Her WNBA career began in 1997, the league's inaugural season, when Boucek played for the Cleveland Rockers. "It's really, really important for someone who moves around a lot to find fellowship when you move to a new city," said Boucek, who was forced to retire as a player after just one WNBA season because of a back injury. "I always try to find some believers that I can spend time with either talking on the phone or sending emails and I make sure I get in God's Word everyday."

When Boucek arrived on the WNBA scene after a successful collegiate career at the University of Virginia, she was looking for answers to some spiritual and life-related questions. Her visits to the team's chapel services helped address those questions. "I was all alone and vulnerable and looking for some stability in a very unstable profession," added Boucek. "The chapels that I attended while I was in Cleveland are what planted the seeds for me. The WNBA was my harvest so I know it is a good harvest."

Boucek now spends her days coaching basketball and sharing God's goodness with others. She knows that there are many young women in need of the same spiritual truths that she began seeking several years ago. "It's an environment where the players go through a lot of highs and a lot of lows," said Boucek. "A lot of them are out on their own for the first time. It's their first job out of college."

Boucek knows her WNBA mission is about more than winning games: it's about winning souls. "As believers we're all ambassadors just dressed as other things and I'm dressed as an assistant coach in the WNBA at the moment," she said. "It's an intense, stressful job at times. I keep my focus on Jesus—representing Him and being a light. It's a challenge, but that's my goal. Our walk is a lot more powerful than our talk, so I'm just trying to say the right thing, do the right thing and be different and let them get curious and be drawn to the light."

Chapter 15

LANCE BERKMAN

Houston Astros, Outfielder

The LORD lifts up the humble...

Psalm 147:6 (NKJV)

During his rise to baseball stardom, Lance Berkman could have easily taken credit for his on-field successes. After a spectacular career at Rice University he was named the 1997 College Baseball Player of the Year. Soon after, he was selected with the 16th overall pick by the Houston Astros. It did not take long for Berkman to move up the minor-league ranks. By 2000, the outfielder had found his way into the Astros starting lineup on a regular basis. Berkman, now a three-time All-Star, has achieved so much and it has humbled him even more. "Everything I have comes from God," he said. "My life is a total blessing. I sit there and think what did I do to deserve the ability to play baseball at this level? And you can say nothing. It's just gifted to you. And when you come to that realization, you're so thankful. There's nothing to brag about or to get a big head about. You just use the tools that God has given you."

Berkman has used those tools well and has consistently ranked among baseball's best. In 2004, he batted .316 and slugged 30 home-runs. The previous season he ripped 42 home-runs and led the National League with 128 runs batted in. While Berkman is always looking for ways to improve his game, he is also busy gaining more knowledge about his faith in Christ by taking classes from the College of Biblical Studies in Houston. Whether it is on the field or away from it, Berkman does everything with boundless enthusiasm. "The key in athletics and with your walk with the Lord is that consistent, day in and day out performance," said Berkman. "In baseball you have to continue to produce and the guys who do are the ones considered to be the good players because they are consistent. With Christ, the consistent walk is the one that keeps you out of trouble. If you don't have it, you're probably going to end up failing more times than you should because you haven't prepared yourself to face the challenges that are out there on a daily basis."

Raised in a Christian household, it was during his collegiate career that Berkman realized the need to recommit his life to Jesus Christ. Now his focus is as much on the mission field as it is on the baseball field. "We're all missionaries in everyday life, and not always in words, but deeds are more important," he said. "It's just showing people that you care and that you love them. Becoming a servant is something the Lord has been showing me. Even for the guy who's riding high to become a servant. They may never ask you about it but they may think in the back of their minds, 'what makes that guy so different?' And that's when you have the ability to really impact somebody."

Chapter 16

JOHN SMOLTZ
Atlanta Braves, Pitcher

The things which you learned and received and heard and saw in me, these do, and the God of peace will be with you.

Philippians 4:9 (NKJV)

Atlanta Braves Pitcher John Smoltz is a big believer that actions should speak louder than words. Regarded as one of the best pitchers in baseball, the six-foot, three-inch right-hander has tormented his Major League opponents for more than a decade. In addition to his on-field success, the four-time All-Star has come to understand there is more to life than just trying to strike out the next batter he faces. Before Smoltz committed to a personal relationship with Jesus Christ, he saw things quite differently than he does now. "My rules were I played for me," he said. "Now, it's a different set of rules so that God gets all the glory. I am as competitive as the next person but I don't go to the extreme. I try to live my life so that if no one ever hears me say a word, they watch me and judge me by my actions. If you never heard me say a word you would say there's something special about that guy. He's different."

Smoltz became different through the life-changing power of God that he embraced in 1995. It just so happened that the following season was his best ever. The Lansing,

Michigan native led the majors in wins (24), strikeouts (276) and strikeouts per nine innings (9.8) on his way to being named the winner of the 1996 National League's Cy Young Award. "I'm not saying becoming a Christian got me the Cy Young, but it enabled me to handle all the things that I wouldn't have been able to handle," explained Smoltz. "The success wouldn't have gone to my head, but it would have affected me in ways that I couldn't have handled. That year, I read the book of Philippians over and over just to gain perspective."

Despite injuries that limited his playing time in recent years, Smoltz is focused more than ever on making his best pitch—the one he makes vocally for the Lord every chance he gets. "I never thought I'd get the opportunity to stand in front of 5,000 people to share my testimony or my faith," said Smoltz, who is now back in the starting rotation after being utilized as a relief pitcher for several seasons. Whether through his bold testimony or his blazing fastball, the veteran pitcher does not hold back-regardless of where he is and what he is doing.

"Playing baseball now, the main focus is to do my best," added Smoltz. "I believe that if God was out there on the mound and He had to throw His best knockdown pitch and His best inside pitch it would be just that."

Chapter 17

Paul Byrd
Cleveland Indians, Pitcher

A righteous man may have many troubles, but the LORD delivers him from them all.

Psalm 34:19 (NIV)

Like trying to use his best pitch to find the strike zone, Paul Byrd of the Cleveland Indians knows there is only one real target to aim at. It's the one that keeps him connected to his Lord and Savior, Jesus Christ. "What I'm learning is it isn't enough just to have Jesus in your life, you have to be dependent upon Him," said Byrd. "A lot of people have Jesus in their lives, including me, but I need to be more dependent upon Him, so I'm learning that."

Byrd has been challenged to increase his connection with Christ through tragedy and disappointment. He underwent career-threatening arm surgery after missing the remainder of the 2000 season, then he was shaken by the death of his brother during the following off-season. "The only thing I'm sure of is my son-ship to God and my marriage to Jesus," said Byrd, a former All-American at Louisiana State University. "People say God won't give you more than you can handle. I've never read that verse. He says you'll have trouble. I feel that He gives you more than you can handle so you'll be dependent upon Him. His love for me is amazing and I depend on it every day."

Byrd has never felt God's unconditional love more than during a game in the 1999 season. While pitching for Atlanta, Byrd had just given up a grand slam to slugger Bobby Bonilla and was heading to the dugout after getting pulled from the game. "I walked off the field among the boo's and while I didn't hear the voice audibly, I was told: 'hold your head up high, you're My child, a child of God. You're My son.' It enabled me to hold my head up and walk off and it didn't matter what anybody thought. I've needed to know that through an inconsistent career."

The high point of Byrd's professional career came during that same season. The veteran right-hander was selected to play in his first All-Star game after ranking among the National League leaders in several categories. Accolades are great, but Byrd has received something far greater than any worldly treasure—a crown of righteousness that comes only from God.

In 1992, before giving his life to Christ, Byrd was playing in the minor leagues. He recalls the void he experienced at that time: "When you get behind closed doors, you know you're empty.

You know you're thirsty for something. You know that the game with all the fame and money can't fill that void either. What God gives you is permanent and it's what you're looking for because He created you and He knows what's missing."

Chapter 18

Orel Hershiser
Texas Rangers, Pitching Coach

God is faithful, by whom you were called into the fellowship of His Son, Jesus Christ our Lord.

1 Corinthians 1:9 (NKJV)

During his successful career as a Major League pitcher, Orel Hershiser earned the nickname "Bulldog." It was for good reason: He squared off against his opponents with a relentless tenacity. It was with the same zeal that he embraced his relationship with God. But since retiring in 2000, Hershiser has found that his approach to his walk with Jesus Christ has changed, just as his career has. "The reasons are a bit different than how I was motivated before," said Hershiser, now pitching coach for the Texas Rangers. "It's important for me not to think that just because I was in the public eye that I was accountable and responsible and held up to a certain level. Now that I'm not in the public eye—in the background in a coaching job—I need to continue to work on my relationship on a daily basis to continue to be close to the Lord and always understanding God's love."

With the Los Angeles Dodgers in 1988, Hershiser was baseball's top pitcher. He won the Cy Young Award and led the league in victories, complete games and innings pitched. The following season, he set a Major League record by pitching 59 consecutive scoreless innings. Even after experiencing setbacks with arm injuries, Hershiser went on to enjoy several successful seasons with Cleveland, San Francisco and the New York Mets before his retirement. "It's great to still be around baseball and to have those friendships," added Hershiser. "It's important to have that accountability and to have that fellowship with different people."

Hershiser knows the importance of relationships and how vital they are, especially when a ballplayer has retired or the season has ended. "We can be very season-oriented as far as our friendships," said Hershiser. "For me, the close-knit bonds from church, church friends and friends from over the years keep me accountable and responsible to keep the straight and narrow."

Hershiser accepted Jesus Christ as his Lord and Savior in 1979 at the age of 21. Like developing his repertoire of pitches, one of baseball's best pitchers says his maturity in Christ also took time and diligence through seeking God's Word, praying and spending time with other

Christians. "To develop, what I would say a mature relationship, it might have been about three, four, even five years," said Hershiser. "It's maybe in the last 20 years that I've begun to understand the depth of God's love and what it's like to walk with Him on a daily basis and know His wisdom."

Hershiser is still focused on making his best pitch—for Jesus Christ.

Chapter 19

Betsy King

Ladies Professional Golf Association (LPGA) Tour, Hall of Fame Golfer

I have been crucified with Christ; it is no longer I who live, but Christ lives in me; and the life which I now live in the flesh I live by faith in the Son of God, who loved me and gave Himself for me.

Galatians 2:20 (NKJV)

Betsy King remembers January 1980. It was at the beginning of her third year on the Ladies Professional Golf Association Tour and she had made the biggest and best decision of her life by asking Jesus Christ to be her Lord and Savior. "It took that kind of pressure for me to be reached and for me to understand that I can't do everything," said King. "I saw that I needed the Lord in my life and that I wasn't all self-sufficient. The pressure of playing tournament golf had gotten me to that point."

After King made that decision, she felt the burden lifted off her shoulders and experienced a sense of peace. King's personal life was great, but the same could not be said for her golf game. "I had my worst year on tour," she said. "I had people say to me, 'you've lost your competitive edge, you're a Christian and you don't seem to take it as seriously as you should.' It probably took me a little while to find the balance."

Finding balance did not take long at all. King found a new teacher to help with her game and her level of play began to escalate. "God rewarded me that way just for being faithful in that first year," added King. She proceeded to notch 28 victories from 1984 to 1992 and, upon winning her 30th (the ShopRite Classic in 1995), she was inducted into the LPGA Hall of Fame. King has won six major tournament titles and amassed many honors, including LPGA Tour Player of the Year three times. Making Christ the focus of her life has been the key to keeping her career in proper perspective. "I have to say that's a constant challenge," said King. "Because when you're a professional athlete many people interact with you based on how you perform. It's a constant struggle to keep that in perspective. I always like to say 'God loves me the same whether I shoot 68 or 80.' It's a constant lesson I have to remind myself about particularly when I do have a bad day on the course."

In 1998, King also became the first player in LPGA history to pass the six-million dollar mark in career earnings. King has much to be thankful for and shows her appreciation by using every possible opportunity to glorify God and share His goodness with others. "It's a great platform," said King. "And I don't mind being on a platform in trying to use the success that I've had to reach others for Christ."

Chapter 20

Bob Gilder

Champions Tour, Professional Golfer

For the things which are seen are temporary, but the things which are not seen are eternal.

2 Corinthians 4:18 (NKJV)

Whether Bob Gilder is facing the toughest hole on the golf course or yet another obstacle in the game of life, the veteran golfer knows how to take his best swing. "My parents became Christians when I was in high school and I gave my life to the Lord when I was in college at Arizona State," said Gilder, who began his career at the school as a walk-on. He went on to become the Western Athletic Conference Golf Champion and earned honorable mention All-American. "It's been a great relationship with Christ. I couldn't do it without Him."

Gilder has also enjoyed his fair share of success as a professional golfer. He won seven times on the Professional Golfers' Association (PGA) Tour between 1976 and 1982, notching three victories in 1982 alone. Since arriving on the Champion's Tour scene, Gilder has posted seven wins, including the 2001 Senior Tour Championship. At the 2003 Emerald Coast Classic, he carded the best tournament score on the tour that year and shattered the previous record by three strokes. Yet, the success pales in comparison to his quest for reaching the ultimate target. "This is all going to go away," added Gilder. "Winning golf tournaments and major championships is fun while you're doing it but it means nothing when compared to long range goals. It's where you're going to be for eternity that makes a difference. If you're not working toward that end and working toward other people seeing that, then you're not doing your work."

With no shortage of on-course hazards and plenty of distractions, it is easy to see the similarities between golf and life. Gilder spends plenty of time in Bible study, Friday night chapel service and with his fellow believers on tour to make sure he is prepared for the challenges that are sure to come his way. "You can't do this by yourself," said Gilder, "If you're doing it by yourself then you're doing it for the wrong person."

Golf is full of surprises, with no shortage of bad breaks and bounces. Even in the heat of competition, Gilder is always conscious of being an ambassador for Christ. "I believe we're out there to glorify God, through our actions and our speech," he said. "And if you're not doing that then you're thinking about the wrong things."

Gilder is committed to staying on course on his way to claiming the greatest prize of all: The crown of life.

Chapter 21

DAVID GOSSETT

Professional Golfers' Association (PGA) Tour, Professional Golfer

You will go out in joy and be led forth in peace.
       Isaiah 55:12 (NIV)

In the midst of the great success he was experiencing during his collegiate golf career at the University of Texas, David Gossett discovered that something was missing. It wasn't a technique in his swing that would keep him from winning more titles or prevent him from competing at the highest level of golf. No, this was a far more serious matter. "Life was looking good to me," the 1999 U.S. Amateur Champion said. "Yet no matter how much success I had, it just didn't fill the void in my heart. I saw the peace in people's lives who walked with the Lord and I wanted it."

Through attending on-campus meetings for the Fellowship of Christian Athletes and Champions for Christ, Gossett got what he needed: the gift of salvation through Jesus Christ and the peace and joy that he had long sought. Raised in a Christian environment, Gossett described himself as someone who 'tried to do the right thing and, by worldly standards, was a good kid.' Coming to an understanding of God's grace was pivotal. "God is a forgiving God and a loving God and He's always there for us," Gossett said.

Nowadays, Gossett is one of the young, up and coming players on the Professional Golfers' Association (PGA) Tour. After becoming the first player to shoot a 59 at Tour Qualifying, Gossett earned his way onto the PGA Tour and during his 2001 rookie season, in just his 11th PGA Tour event, won the John Deere Classic. He is currently climbing to the top of the winning list and, more importantly, into a deeper, personal relationship with God. "I'm just so pleased to be out here, to have gifts and talents that He's given me and somehow use them to His pleasing. My life is in His hands. He's directing my paths. No matter how much I want to gain control and direct the ship, He's the wind that puts the sail. I'm thankful that Jesus is who He says He is. He is truth and life. That's exciting. I want to work on having that joyful peace that God brings."

Like spending time perfecting his swing at the practice range, Gossett now knows that getting God's fullest means spending time with Christ, the author and finisher of our faith. "The best way I can get close to Him is to spend time in His Word," he added. "So much scripture talks about spending time in His Word. The more I read the more I sense His presence and there's harmony in my life through my attitudes and actions."

Chapter 22

LEAH O'BRIEN-AMICO
U.S. Women's Olympic Softball Team

The LORD is my rock and my fortress and my deliverer; My God, my strength, in whom I will trust;...
Psalm 18:2 (NKJV)

During her college days as a three-time All-American at the University of Arizona, Leah O'Brien-Amico was by softball standards a "can't miss" prospect. She batted an amazing .428 and helped lead the Wildcats to three National Collegiate Athletic Association (NCAA) Championships. However, when it came to developing a serious commitment to living her life for Christ, O'Brien-Amico swung and missed. "I used to think I was a Christian but I only went through the motions," said O'Brien-Amico. "I would pray but I never saw anything happen in my life. As I truly, truly trusted in Jesus Christ and said, 'Lord, I want you to take control of my entire life,' I have seen Him work in my life as well as the lives of others."

That commitment came after she accepted an invitation to an on-campus Bible study. Since then, O'Brien-Amico's life has changed dramatically. In the summer of 2004, as the starter at first base for the United States Women's Olympic Softball Team, she helped the team notch its third straight Olympic gold medal. All during this time she was not only married to husband Tommy but also mother to young son Jake. "I definitely had days when I said, 'there's just no way I can do this,'" added O'Brien-Amico. "I looked at the challenging schedule that I had for the 2004 Olympic year and the commitments that we had—the training, the time in the weight room, the running and all the other things. Also, to be the best wife and mother I could be, I knew that I had to keep trusting in Jesus and He would allow it all to work out with my son and my husband. They were my support group when I went into the Olympic Games."

Far beyond the thrill of winning another gold medal, O'Brien-Amico is even more excited in knowing that God has positioned her to share the Gospel with others. "I see Him moving in the hearts of the other players," said O'Brien-Amico. "I always see people asking a lot of questions and I think it's helping me to grow as well so I can come to them with answers. I see people wanting to know more about Jesus. Each day, when I go out there with my teammates, I want to be the best on the field and I'm constantly reminded that I have to continue to trust in Him or it's not going to work out the right way."

With that perspective, O'Brien-Amico is hitting a grand slam for Jesus.

Chapter 23

CATHERINE "CAT" REDDICK
U.S. Olympic Soccer, Defender

Now to him who is able to do immeasurably more than all we ask or imagine, according to his power that is at work within us...
Ephesians 3:20 (NIV)

Playing alongside and against the best women soccer players in the world, Catherine "Cat" Reddick sometimes asks herself the question, "why am I here?" Reddick, however, is more than deserving of her position among the nation's elite athletes. Arguably the best and youngest up-and-coming player in the country, Reddick's brilliant play as a defender earned her a spot on the U.S. Olympic Team, which captured a gold medal at the 2004 Games in Athens, Greece. "Playing with these girls is an amazing experience," said Reddick. "God's put me here for a reason and I just have to keep honoring Him. That's how I have to focus. Soccer is sort of my sanctuary, my place to worship Him, so I look at it that way."

As you can imagine, playing in this highly competitive environment is difficult. Reddick knows that remaining humble is her biggest test. "He's always been working on humility with me," added the former All-American at the University of North Carolina, who helped the Tar Heels notch a perfect record and the NCAA championship in 2003. "I think right now I keep trying to stay focused on being humble towards Him, because there've been so many times that there have been disappointments and I've wanted what I didn't get. He's taught me to be humble and to really keep my focus on Him."

Reddick says she is fortunate to have been raised in a Christian household. Her father is an associate pastor at a church and God's Word has been laid as the foundation in her life. Because of that, Reddick does not let her youth keep her from confidently sharing her faith in Jesus Christ, even with the veteran players on the U.S. Team. "If the conversation gets brought up, I'm the first one to jump in," said Reddick. "If someone starts talking about God, I tell them that Jesus is the only way to Heaven. Mostly, I try to let my actions do the talking. They might see my purity ring and ask me why I'm waiting until I am married. I tell them, 'that's the way I was brought up and that's the way the Lord says to do it.'"

Just like in soccer, Reddick also knows that putting forth a half-hearted effort in her relationship with Christ is not enough. When she does not spend enough time reading God's Word and praying, it shows. "There's always times when you go through the motions and that's when the walk is always the hardest," she added. "And you wonder why your life isn't as good as it used to be and it's because you're not focused on God."

Chapter 24

MATT JORDAN

Colorado Rapids, Goalkeeper

In the same way, let your light shine before men, that they may see your good deeds and praise your Father in heaven.

Matthew 5:16

Simply put, Matt Jordan is one of Major League Soccer's (MLS) best goalies. While playing for Dallas in 2001, his nine shutouts earned him a tie for the league lead. Two years earlier, Jordan's 1.08 goals-against average set a team record and ranked second best in MLS. When it comes to soccer, Jordan, the 10th overall selection in the 1998 MLS college draft, has rarely allowed opponents to reach the goal. In life, his greatest quest is to see others score life's biggest prize—a personal relationship with Jesus Christ.

"I really believe that being a leader by example is the best way for me to share my faith," said Jordan, now back in his home state as a member of the Colorado Rapids. "I've found that a lot of people look at the way I live my life, the way I conduct myself and the way I handle myself out on the field. That's how I can best reach people, by leading by example. That is my way of blessing others."

Just as Jordan faces difficulty on the soccer field, life also presents its share of problems. Jordan uses the same Biblical principles to emerge victoriously. "I go through just as many troubled times as anybody," added Jordan, a former standout at Clemson University. "People think that just because you're an athlete you are untouchable. But a lot of times, you're more vulnerable. I'm really blessed, though, because I'm in a profession that's really pure and I'm able to use my God-given gifts on a daily basis."

Jordan, the Colorado High School Player of the Year in 1994, could easily get caught up in his accomplishments. But the six-two, 185 pound goalkeeper is constantly reminded of the peace and joy he has when he keeps himself focused on being led by the Lord. "My daily focus is to let go and let God take over," said Jordan. "It's not easy sometimes because you feel like you want to have control of things. If you approach everything that you do, whether it's on the field or off the field and you do things according to His Word, the rest falls into place."

Generally, that means another opponent's kick kept out of the goal and another day living in the Lord's presence. "I feel God's joy when I do my best with the gifts that He's blessed me with."

Chapter 25

ADAM BURT

National Hockey League, Defenseman (Former)

And whatever you do, do it heartily, as to the Lord and not to men.
Colossians 3:23 (NKJV)

Playing in the sometimes violent sport of hockey, it would have been easy to ask Adam Burt: What is a nice guy like you doing in a game like this? "Being a Christian athlete playing a physical sport, where fighting is involved in the parameters of the game, there is a very fine line," said Burt, a former National Hockey League defenseman. "It's kind of funny because, a lot of times, if you aren't a physical player you become one of these wimpy Christian guys and if you are physical you become hypocritical, so to speak. Myself, I have always been of the mindset, whatever you do, do it heartily unto the Lord. As long as your heart is right and there's no malice there, you should go out there and play with a great deal of intensity."

Burt, who spent 13 years in the National Hockey League, began his career in Hartford. He also played for Carolina and Philadelphia. Over a period of time, he learned how to deal with the challenges that came with being a follower of Christ while playing the sport he loves. That, however, does not imply that Burt always did it perfectly. "I'd like to say I was never out there sinning but I can't," added Burt. "Not only did the players on the other team try to goad me, the players on my team were watching to see how I would react. There were times on the ice when I got frustrated and slipped up."

It was during a family crisis in his early teens when Burt gave his life to Jesus Christ. He continues to see God shape him in many areas of his life. "I tried to find my identity in being a professional athlete," said Burt, who played for Team USA in the 1993 World Championships. "I knew about having Jesus as my Savior, but I didn't understand Lordship until I fell flat on my face several times trying to do things in my own strength and on my own power. Finally God beat it through my head that Jesus is Lord as well. And you know what? My life's a lot better with Him in control."

Christianity is not something most people associate with the sport of hockey. While the number of believers is proportionately smaller than in many other sports, Burt remains excited about the possibilities. "I look at hockey and I can get a little jealous sometimes because it's not there. But in the same breath we can say, 'look at the opportunity for growth there.' For the most part, there are a lot of guys who've never heard the Gospel. With it being an international sport, there's an opportunity to impact the whole world."

Chapter 26

Darrell Waltrip
NASCAR Hall of Fame Inductee

...so that I may finish my race with joy, and the ministry which I received from the Lord Jesus, to testify to the gospel of the grace of God.

Acts 20:24 (NKJV)

Growing up in Owensboro, Kentucky, Darrell Waltrip's focus was on reaching the winner's circle. It began with go-kart racing when he was 12. His dream was to advance to the pinnacle of stock car racing success. "That was my mission," said Waltrip. "I pursued that with everything that I had."

By 1972, after establishing himself on dirt tracks and short tracks, Waltrip made his National Association of Stock Car Auto Racing (NASCAR) debut at Alabama's Talladega Speedway. Three years later, he decided to shift gears and hit the track full-time in order to face the world's best drivers on the NASCAR Winston Cup Series.

The rest is racing history. Checkered flags along with fame and fortune soon followed as Waltrip quickly rose to the ranks of one of the sport's elite drivers. Everything seemed to be going just as planned. That was until one day in 1983 when, at the urging of his wife, Stevie, he attended an event near their home in Nashville, Tennessee and listened to a minister discuss eternal life. "I thought that if I was a good guy I would go to heaven if anything ever happened to me," explained Waltrip, who was NASCAR's Driver of the Decade in the 1980s. "I figured if I got killed in a race car...I was a good person. I never killed anybody. I never robbed anybody. I figured I'd go to heaven."

Waltrip, seeing his need for a Savior, surrendered his life to Jesus Christ. Stevie had already begun her walk with the Lord and was a great encourager to her husband and others at the race track. "She was attending Bible study fellowship and got on fire for the Lord and started working on me," said Waltrip, a three-time Winston Cup Series Champion. "In our sport there's an element of danger and she wanted to make sure every Sunday that I was protected the best I, and the other drivers, could be."

It became a race day custom that Stevie would hand out note cards containing Bible scriptures to the drivers. The Waltrip's took another giant step in 1986, teaming up with several other racing couples to form Motor Racing Outreach. "We saw a huge need on the circuit," said Waltrip. "It's our church at the track."

After retiring in 2001 and being inducted into

the NASCAR Hall of Fame, Waltrip still stays connected to the sport as a television analyst. Looking back, he sees how powerfully he has been used to share God's love with others. "Sports give us such a great platform," he said. "I'm glad that I can do my part and I wish other guys would step up and do the same thing."

Chapter 27

Ezra Lusk

Motorcycle Racer

He who dwells in the shelter of the Most High will rest in the shadow of the Almighty. I will say of the LORD, "He is my refuge and my fortress, my God, in whom I trust."

Psalm 91:1-2 (NIV)

To fans of motocross and supercross racing, Ezra Lusk is a household name. Considered one of the sport's premier riders, Lusk has amassed dozens of championships and honors since he turned professional in 1992. Ever since he began riding at five years old, Lusk aspired to be the best. "That's what drove me through life, pretty much, to be that number one guy," he said. "But you get up to that level and you have to handle not winning, not being the best. At one point, I couldn't handle it."

Lusk needed something to change in his life. During the 2000 racing season, the transformation began to take place. First, he met his wife Jennifer. Then, he came in contact with a chaplain through Motor Racing Outreach, a ministry that helps racers with their spiritual needs. Soon after, Lusk, who grew up going to church but admits to only going through the motions up to that point, saw the need to re-commit his life to Jesus Christ. "Now, my number one focus everyday is the Lord," added Lusk, who won a total of nine major events in 1998 and 1999. "Once I started doing that, things haven't changed as far as my results go but I didn't think it would. I'm a lot happier now. If I would quit racing tomorrow and not have accomplished my goals, there are other things that Christ is going to help me out with the rest of my life."

For now, racing is what he does. And despite a series of injuries that have forced him to miss some races in recent years, Lusk is still going at full throttle. In a sport where danger is at every turn, the former Amateur National Championship winner enjoys the peace and comfort he can only get from his Heavenly Father. "When I go out there to do what I do, most people think that I would be scared," added Lusk, who became a first-time father in 2003 with the birth of his son, Hayden Patrick. "But I go out there and actually feel safe. I guess, you could say, it's in His hands."

These days, Lusk has put his safety—and his life—in God's hands.

Chapter 28

Pat Day

Hall of Fame Jockey

Then the Spirit lifted me up and brought me into the inner court, and the glory of the LORD filled the temple.

Ezekiel 43:5 (NIV)

For more than two decades it has been a common occurrence to see Pat Day in the winner's circle after a horse race. A four-time Eclipse Award winner, which is given to the jockey of the year, Day knows what it is like to lead the pack. He also knows how it feels to be at the top of his sport and feel unfulfilled. "In my case, the Lord let me get a hold of the brass ring and realize it was tied to nothing," said Day. "I found the pot at the end of the rainbow but it was empty. In that, I mean I experienced tremendous success as a jockey. I was the leading rider in the country in the number of races won and realized, having gotten a hold of that brass ring, it didn't satisfy me. It did not bring the long-term peace, joy and contentment that I thought it would. Recognizing that, it had me looking."

In 1984, Day found what he was looking for in a most unlikely way. In a Miami, Florida hotel the night before a race, Day awakened just minutes after going to sleep. He turned the television back on to see a program where people were answering a challenge to commit their lives to Jesus Christ. "I recognized and realized in that instant that the presence in that room with me was the Spirit of The Living God and this was my personal altar call," added the winner of nine Triple Crown races, including the 1992 Kentucky Derby. "It was like the scales were removed from my eyes and I knew what I needed. What I was looking for was a relationship with God that was available only through Jesus Christ."

As Day continued to notch victories he began to question more and more his future as a jockey, mostly about being in a sport so closely linked to gambling. In 1992, a year after being inducted into the Horse Racing Hall of Fame, Day needed an answer. "I had a bit of a dilemma," he said. "I prayed about it. I sought the scriptures. I sought Godly council and through that process God revealed to me that He had saved me to work within the industry, not to leave it. I am to take the talent, abilities and gifts He has blessed me with and the opportunities He makes available to me. I am to use success as a platform to get people's attention. Then, I give Him all the praise and honor and glory for it."

Hearing his name announced as the winner of a race still brings Day great satisfaction. Nothing however, compares to what he looks forward to hearing when his time comes to see Jesus face to face. Said Day: "My heart's desire, my lifelong goal, is to one day hear Jesus say, 'well done my good and faithful servant.'"

TO MAKE JESUS CHRIST LORD AND SAVIOR OF YOUR LIFE...
Pray this prayer in faith:

Dear Father, I come to you in the name of Jesus. You say when I confess with my mouth and believe in my heart that You are Lord, then I will be saved. I believe that Jesus died on the cross for my sins and rose from the dead. I thank You for making me a new creation in Christ and I promise to live my life for You from this day forward.

Jesus, thank You for coming into my heart, being Lord and Savior of my life, filling me with Your Holy Spirit and giving me eternal life and Your promise of an abundant life on this earth. Amen.

If you prayed this prayer, you have made the greatest decision of your life. This is the start of an exciting journey to eternity with Christ. Find a Bible-believing church, make God's Word the authority in your life, and spend time with others who will encourage you as you grow in your faith.

Please send us a note so we may pray for you and welcome you into God's Kingdom!

Greengard Family Ministries
2250 Gause Blvd., PMB 51089
Slidell, LA 70461

or visit our website at
www.ChristianSportsMinute.com

Printed in the United States
51518LVS00002BA/229-408